The outlying suburbs of Sladebrook and Combe Down.

"Aquae Sulis, Aquae Sulis, sleeping far beneath our feet
Never more shall Roman triumph sound thro' thy deserted street".

JOHN ALLEYNE. "Aquae Sullis" A Somerset anthology 1924.

Pulteney Bridge spanning the River Avon at the city's centre. This is the only example in Bath of the 18th century Scottish Architect, Robert Adam.

BATH
INSPIRED IMAGES

JON DAVISON

To my son Jackson

First published by Inspired Images 1990

Inspired Images
12 New High Street
Headington
Oxford
OX3 7AQ

Tel: 0865 741296
Fax: 0865 750276

Photographs, Design & Art Direction: Jon Davison
Quotations compiled by: Johnny Coppin & Mark Allen
Introduction: Mark Allen
Studio Production: Bob Prescott

ISBN 1 869824 20 4

Printed in Yugoslavia
by Gorenjski Tisk, Kranj

The house of the late Richard 'Bea' Nash, the celebrated social reformist who did much to change the standards of the city of Bath during the early 1700's. The house is now Popjoys Restaurant in Saw Close.

"Up and down the city streets the ghosts of long ago,
Mid the crowds of modern days, wander to and fro".
FLORENCE TYLEE. "Shopping in Bath" 1922.

F O R E W O R D

LONGLEAT HOUSE
WARMINSTER, WILTS, BA12 7NN
Telephone: Maiden Bradley (09853) 551
Fax: (09853) 838

I am very flattered to have been asked to write a foreword to this book on Bath, for it is a city that I have known and loved throughout my life. A city that deserves to be recorded well - and that is what this admirable book has done.

I am not artistic myself, but when I see art I do appreciate quality, and quality plus atmosphere, is what Jon Davison's superb photographs have captured. As I have said - I know Bath well, but Mr. Davison has shown it to me in a new, but ancient, light. I will hurry to revisit, together with the thousands of tourists that are attracted to such a magical city, and guided by this book, will understand much better the close attachment, near love, that I feel for our united names.

Bath

ABOVE: Longleat House was completed by Sir John Thynne in 1580, and has been the home of the Thynne family for over 400 years. Longleats present owner, Henry Frederick Thynne is the 6th Marquess of Bath.
LEFT: The Marquess of Bath by Graham Sutherland.

"A Varie faire, neat, and elegant house, in a foule soile, which although once or twise it hath beene burnt, hath risen eftsoones more faire".

WILLIAM CAMDEN. 'Britain' 1610.

I N T R O D U C T I O N

When the Romans arrived in the West Country shortly after AD 43, they found a well-established shrine where the Celts paid homage to their ancient god, Sullis. With a shrewd combination of power politics and public relations the invading forces erected a fine temple above the miraculous springs and dedicated it jointly to Sullis and the Roman goddess of healing and wisdom, Minerva.

The hot waters were captured within pipes and channelled through a series of capacious, lead-lined baths. Every day, then as now, a quarter of a million gallons of water emerged from the earth at a constant temperature of 46°C to fill the baths and overflow through the out-fall drains into the River Avon. Roman visitors came from all over Britain to bask in the restorative waters. From its origins as little more than a health spa at a remote Roman outpost, a thriving leisure resort and township arose. The Romans called it "Aqua Sullis".

In AD 410, the Roman occupation of Britain acme to an abrupt end. Rome was under attack from Goths, the legions were withdrawn and the Britons left to fend for themselves. Aqua Sullis began to decay… and nature began to reclaim her own.

A succession of churches and monasteries grew up on the marshy land and the Benedictine Monks incorporated the hot springs and the Roman remains into the fabric of their monastic buildings. Over the next ten centuries, fire and pillage destroyed generation after generation of buildings but the springs continued to flow, attracting both visitors and comment. In the 1100s, an anonymous chronicler referred to Bath as "…a city where little springs, through hidden conduits, send up waters heated without human skills or ingenuity from deep in the bowels of the earth… the sick are want to gather there from all over England to wash away their infirmities in the health giving waters".

The power and influence of the monasteries declined over the years. By 1500, the monastic buildings were in a sorry state and the Bishop decided to intervene to restore the Abbey to its former glory. The building which stands today is the result of this work. Created in the Perpendicular Gothic style, its mass dominates the City.

In 1702, Queen Anne of England visited Bath to "take the waters" and in doing so set the scene for a change of fortune. Bath suddenly became the place to be seen. Throughout the eighteenth century a succession of royal visitors came to the city and society flocked to Bath in ever increasing numbers.

At the turn of the century the infrastructure of Bath left much to be desired. There was nowhere to stay, no civilised entertainment and the streets remained unpaved, unlit, and overrun with rats and ruffians. Bath owes its eighteenth century renaissance to the combined energy and talent of three unusual men - Richard "Beau" Nash, the charismatic dandy; Ralph Allen, the driven entrepreneur; and John Wood, the inspired architect.

Upon his appointment as official master of Ceremonies, Nash introduced a programme of social reforms that transformed Bath into a city of charm and elegance. Regular seasons of classical concerts, balls and parties drew gentlefolk to Bath from all over the United Kingdom.

It was Allen, though, who had made one fortune by introducing a revolutionary postage system and another by financing improvements to the Avons' navigable capability, who had the imagination to visualise a Bath planned and rebuilt in the neo-classical style. To make his dreams become reality, Allen opened up the local quarries and devised a tramway system to transport the stone under its own gravity to the River Avon where it could be conveyed by barge to the City.

Allen was fortunate that in John Wood he found a man whose enthusiasm and skill as an architect matched his own verve as an entrepreneur. Together they shared a vision of the future. Wood drew his inspiration from Roman and Palladian principles. He linked the squares with the crescents and the crescents with the circus so they became a living entity. He embellished the buildings with delicate wrought iron work. He faced the grand houses in a soft white local stone that glowed golden in the summer sunshine... and around the buildings he landscaped lawns and planted shady trees.

By the end of the eighteenth century Nash, Allen and Wood and their successors had transformed the City into the show piece that it remains today.

The overflow from the Roman's sacred spring flows into the River Avon at a rate of 250,000 gallons per day and at a constant temperature of 46.5 degrees.

"Hot streams poured forth over the clear grey stone
To the round pool and down into the baths".
ANON. From 'The Ruin' 8th century translation.

"May the 'White Hart' outrun the 'Bear'
And make the 'Angel' fly
Turn the 'White Lion' upside down
And drink the 'Three Tuns' dry".

OLD TOASTING RHYME IN THE COACHING DAYS.

HOT TUB PUB
COURAGE
THE
HOT TUB PUB
Cafe-Bar-Restaurant
Beers-Wines-Spirits-Teas
OPEN
ALL DAY

Local street artist Jamie Roberts recording the movement of visitors in the Abbey Churchyard.

"I think that art has something to do with an arrest of attention in the midst of distraction".

SAUL BELLOW. 'Writers at Work'.

The imposing facade of Bath Abbey, built in the early 16th century (photographed here on Christmas Eve, 1989).

ABOVE: The grandiose panorama of the Circus, designed by the Bath architect, John Wood in 1765. The Circus is linked by Brock Street to the Royal Crescent. OPPOSITE: Detail of ironwork in Great Putleney Street.

"Solid, cosy, well-to-do, and correct', it seems to sum up the British ideal".

H.M. BATEMAN. 'Bath past and present' 1939.

W·D·LANE
ABBEY DAIRY
TO THE
HOT SPRINGS
AND
ROMAN BATHS
GOOD
FOOD
BATH CITY
MARKETS
by Royal Charter MCLXXXIX

NEW THEATRE ROYAL
DIEU ET MON DROIT

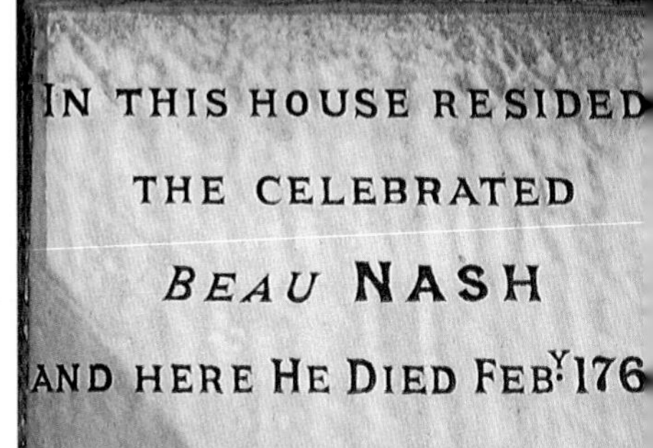
IN THIS HOUSE RESIDED
THE CELEBRATED
BEAU NASH
AND HERE HE DIED FEBY 176

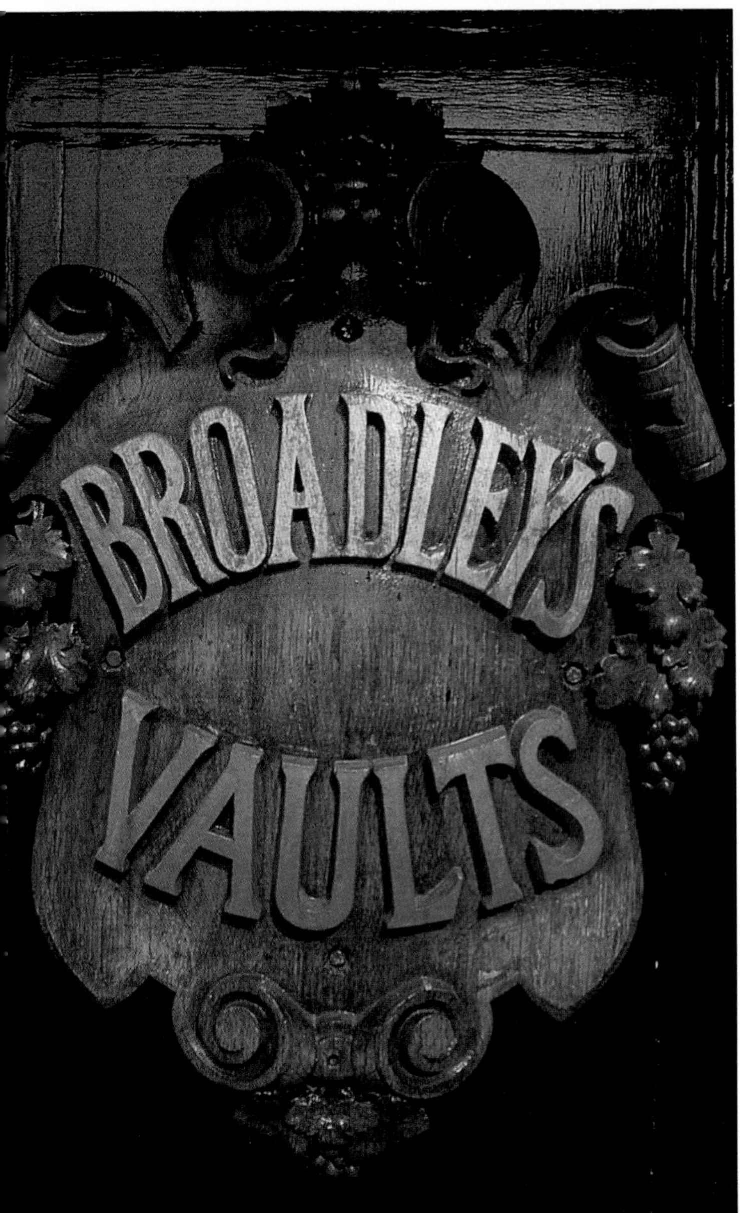
BROADLEY'S
VAULTS

CITY·OF·BATH·COLLEGE
OF FURTHER EDUCATION

WEDDING
AND
PORTRAIT
PHOTOGRAPHY
118

Summer in Bath. The streets are alive with movement, colour and sound. OPPOSITE: A regular street performer during the summer season is Noel Britten's "The Essence of Eccentricity" shows, seen in the Abbey Churchyard.

"Well 'tis a curious place, to say the least ... and it must be a curious people that live therein".

THOMAS HARDY. 'Far from the Madding Crowd' 1874.

ABBEY GALLERIES 9

The launch of the Bath International Festival. This annual event is a city-wide cultural expose of Music and the Arts, and is always accompanied by a stylish start to the festivities. Here John Clifford of Bath's Spa Balloons, leads a launch over the panorama of the Royal Crescent.

OPPOSITE: Pulteney Bridge. This 18th century bridge is based on an Italian design, with integral shops and galleries on either side of the roadway much like the Ponte Veccio in Florence. ABOVE: The interior of the Sunburst Oriental rug house on Argyle Street.

"The graceful bridge with bright little shops full of 'Presents from Bath'".

H.G. WELLS. Secret places of the heart, 1933.

The 100 foot wide avenue of Great Pulteney Street stretches from Argyle Street to the Holburne of Menstrie Museum.
OPPOSITE: York Street lies just behind the Roman Baths, off Kingston Parade.

"Some come here for pleasure, and others for health,
Some come here to squander, and some to get wealth".
WILLIAM CONGREVE. Miscellaneous papers, 1728.

CAFE
POLICE

The Great Roman Bath was enearthed in 1755, when workmen were demolishing the original Abbey Priory. In the background is the medieval bulk of Bath Abbey.

The interior of the Grand Pump Room, and RIGHT: The exterior seen through the entrance to the Abbey Church Yard.

The domed roof of the Concert Room. This room was an extension to the Pump Room and was added in 1897.

"Have you drank the waters, Mr Weller?" inquired his companion, as they walked towards the High St.
"Once," replied Sam.
"What do you think of 'em sir?"
"I thought they wos particklery unpleasant," replied Sam.
"Ah," said Mr John Smauker, "you disliked the Killibeate taste, perhaps?"
"I don't know much about that 'ere," said Sam, "I thought they'd a wery strong flavour o' warm flat irons."
CHARLES DICKENS, The Posthumous Papers of the Pickwick Club, 1837.

OPPOSITE: Choristers about to enter the West doors of the Abbey. These richly carved doors were donated by Sir Henry Montague in 1617 the brother to the then Bishop.

LEFT & BELOW: Angels ascending (and one descending) Jacob's Ladder on the west face of the Abbey.

ABOVE: The Abbey Churchyard. ABOVE RIGHT: The Pump Rooms north front in the Abbey Churchyard. The Greek inscription reads: (water is best).

"As for Bath, all history went and bathed and drank there".
W.M. THACKERAY. From Lecture II of 'The Four Georges'.

ΑΡΙΣΤΟΝ ΜΕΝ ΥΔΩΡ

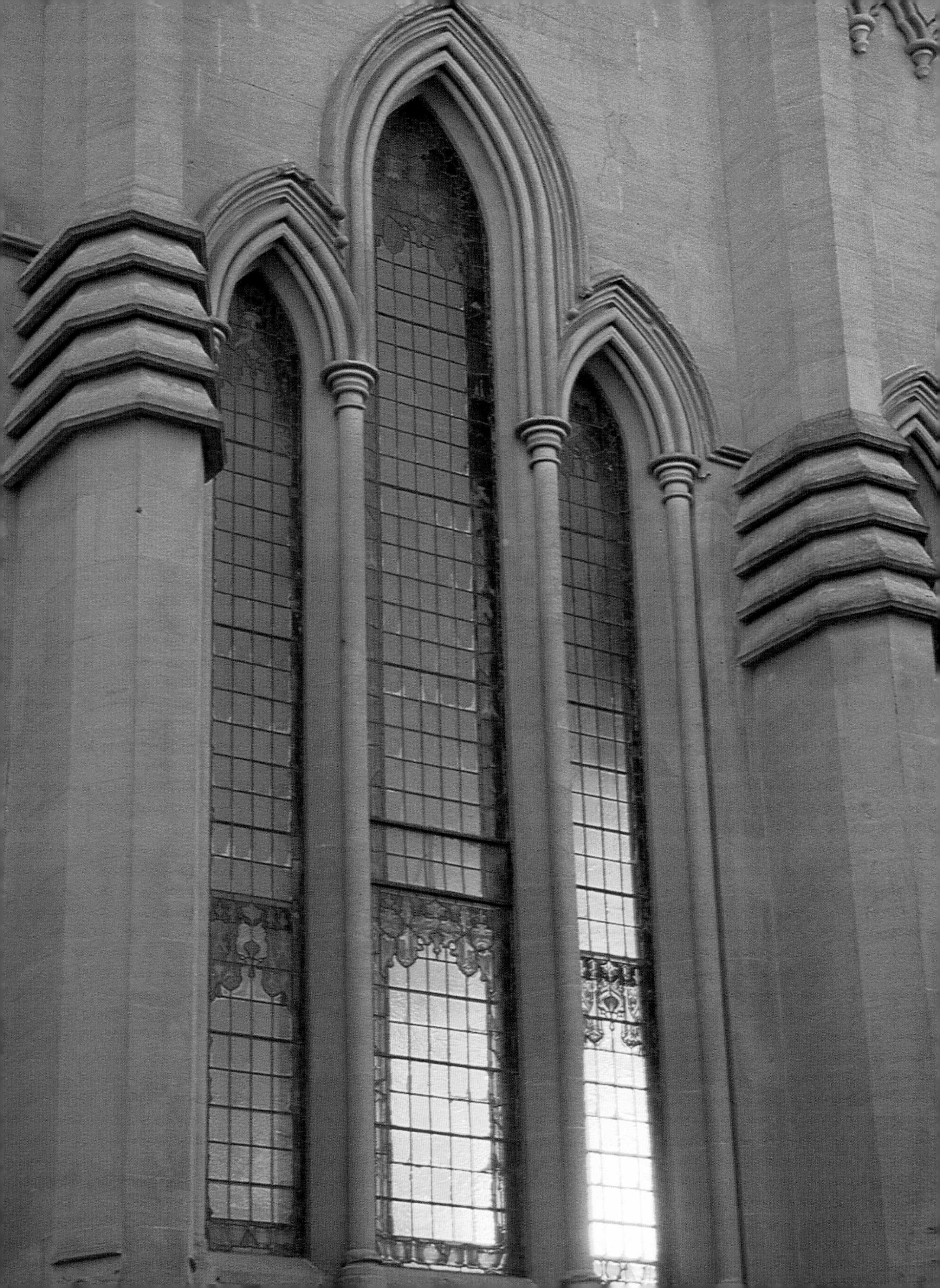

ABOVE: Late spring sunset over houses in Holloway overlooking Beechen Cliff. OPPOSITE: Sunset seen through the Oriel windows of the parish church of St. Michael with St. Paul's on the corner of Walcott Street and Broad Street.

"Bath is decidedly the prettiest town in all England".

THOMAS CARLYLE. 1850.

ABOVE: The great sweep of the Royal Crescent, seen here from the Royal Victoria Park. OPPOSITE: Houses in Upper Church Street.

"The houses are so elegant, the streets are so beautiful, the prospects so enchanting ... ".

FRANCES BURNEY. From 'Arrival at Bath', 1780.

"It is supplied with best provisions of all kinds – and that in plenty".

JOHN WOOD. Advertising Map, 1735.

WHOLE-FOODS
WE SELL THE GOODLIFE
HERBS + SPICES
BEANS PEAS LENTILS
RICE + GRAINS
CEREALS + MUESLI
NUTS + SEEDS
FRUIT
FLOUR + meals
OILS
VINEGARS
SPREADS:
PRESERVES
HONEY
PEANUT BUTTER
TAHINI
MOLASSES
YEAST EXTRACT
+ NIBBLES
PRODUCTS,
BREAD,
CAKES
+ LOTS MORE!
WE SELL
Gillards
TEAS

48p
MANGO
90p
EACH
CONFERENCE PEARS

HILTON

The city from Beechen Cliff looking along Walcot Street towards Hedgemead Park in the distance.

ABOVE: Houses in Holloway on the edge of Alexandra Park, Beechen Cliff. OPPOSITE: A compressed view along the Parragon with Beechen Cliff in the distance.

"It is, in a rather special sense, ancient and modern".
G.K. CHESTERTON. Generally Speaking, 1928.

Houses in the Parragon (left) and Guinea Lane (right), the latter borders Hedgemead Park.

BATH

Pulteney Bridge looking towards Laura Place and Great Pulteney Street, Christmas Eve.

The Circus.

TOP: Queens Lane and Trim Bridge.

The Theatre Royal in Saw Close, next door to Popjoys Restaurant.

"I like Bath, it has quality".
H.V. MORTON. In Search of England, 1927.

Part of the retaining wall at Hedgemead Park. This was built after a disasterous landslide in the late 1800's destroyed part of a suburb that occupied this site. The 'Castle' is a piece of artistic licence, and not part of an old city wall.

"Not but what Bath buguiles me. Taste and measure
of buscuit-coloured stone in curve and square".
LOUIS MACNEICE, Autumn Sequel, 1953.

Ralph Allen's 'Sham Castle' built in 1762 overlooks the city from Bathampton Down, by the Golf Course.

St Marks Community Centre – Lyncombe.

UPRA
est.
1947
DOLLIN
& DAINES
Katherine
Stuart
Jewellery

OPPOSITE: North Parade Passage leads from Abbey Green to York Street.

The walkway around the periphery of Alexandra Park overlooks the city from Beechen Cliff.

"Of all the gay places the world can afford,
By gentle and simple for pastime adored.
Fine balls, and fine concerts, fine buildings, and springs,
Walks, and fine views, and a thousand fine things ... ".

CHRISTOPHER ANSTEY. From 'The New Bath Guide', 1766.

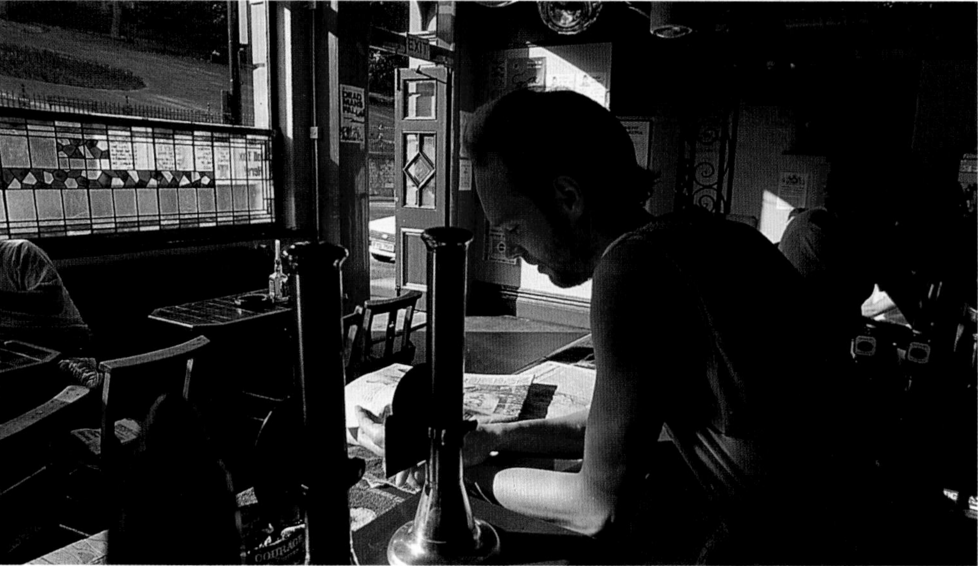

TOP: Walcot Street ABOVE: The recently completed 'Podium' shopping precinct in Walcot Street.

Looking down Gay Street from the Circus.

"To the gay and youthful of both sexes, it is a paradise;
to men in years, a most comfortable retreat".

PHILIP THICKNESSE. The New Prose Bath Guide, 1778.

Pulteney Bridge and the Weir taken from Grand Parade.

"How many generations lingered here to watch the swans above the weir?
How many more will pass this way, dream awhile, and wish to stay?"
JOHN TOMKINS. 'Pulteney Bridge' from Portraits of Bath, 1976.

ABOVE: The Royal Crescent.
OPPOSITE: The festive start to the International Bath Festival. Fireworks from the Royal Crescent mark the end of the first day.
RIGHT: The second day of festivities at the Crescent is marked by the launch of a dozen or more balloon ascents.

TOP: The massive circular structure of the Circus can be found at the top of Gay Street (up the hill). The Circus was designed in 1754 by the Architect John Woods who also designed the Royal Crescent. Woods died before the Circus was completed and it was left to his son to finish the great work. The island in the centre of the Circus is adorned with massive Plane trees. This was once a reservoir which supplied the nearby buildings with water.

The entrance to Royal Victoria Park from Royal Avenue. The Victoria Obelisk was erected in 1837 and commemorates Queen Victoria's 18th birthday. This obelisk was subsequently used to record Victoria's progress through life up to her death in 1901.

"Bath is a spot of ground which our country ought to esteem as a particular favour of heaven".

DANIEL DEFOE. 'A note on Bath'.

Part of the suburb of South Twerton.

TOP: The Podium shopping precinct in Walcot Street. ABOVE: Feeding time, Grand Parade. LEFT: Wrought Iron railings in the Royal Crescent.

TOP: Abbey Green, looking towards the Abbey along North Parade Passage. ABOVE: North Parade passage. RIGHT: Part of the underfloor Hypocaust in the Roman Baths. OPPOSITE: The Roman Baths (the Great Bath).

Part of suburban Oldfield.

TOP: John Clifford from the Spa Balloon company giving pre-flight instructions to his passengers during the Bath Festival.

"Bath is to me a new world; all is gaiety, good humour and diversion..."

TOBIAS SMOLLETT, 1771.

TOP: Shires yard shopping precinct.
ABOVE: Local singer/songwriter Johnny Coppin.
OPPOSITE: Andy Philips, a regular 'Street Entertainer' at the Abbey Churchyard.

"Now houses are 'units' and people are digits
And Bath has been planned for quarters and midgets.
Official designs are aggressively neuter
The puritan work work of an eyeless computer.
Goodbye to old Bath! We who loved you are sorry
They're carting yo off by developer's lorry".
JOHN BETJEMAN, 'The Newest Bath Guide' in 'A Nip in the Air.' 1947.

ABOVE & LEFT: The city Gasworks sandwiched between Upper and Lower Bristol Roads (A4 & A36). TOP: The Royal Crescent.

TOP: The Abbey from Winchcombe Hill. ABOVE: Evening watch, Winchcombe Hill. LEFT: St Steven's Church on Beacon Hill.

Lansdown Crescent built in the late 1700's is considered to combine the essence of the Georgian ideal, Classical architecture and rural simplicity.

"Beneath us, tier on tier, the city falls".

L.B. GRIFFITHS. 'Bath from Lansdown Heights', 1924.

Prior Park, another example of the handiwork of John Wood the elder. The mansion dates from 1735 and was commissioned by Ralph Allen. The mansion is now a Catholic Co-educational school.

The 18th century south front of Widcombe Manor, and its Venetian bronze fountain

"Bath, built of white stone, in trim streets, enclosed amid guarded, beautifully green and feathered hills, looked altogether princely after those poor brick towns... ".

THOMAS CARLYLE. From a letter, 1843.

ACKNOWLEDGEMENTS

The publishers would like to thank the following people for their help and ethusiasm on this project:

Grateful thanks to The Marquess of Bath.

Mrs Linda Gallagher and Eddie Stansby for 'The Lights of Longleat'.

David McLaughlin, Conservation Architect for the Department of the Environmental Services, Bath City Council.

Norman Ellis, our guide at the Roman Baths.

Albert (Ben) Braga, our thanks for the flares at short notice.

John Clifford of the Spa Balloon Company, for a unique view of the city.

Johnny Coppin, as always for the words and music.

PHOTOGRAPHIC NOTES

The images in this book were all captured on Fuji colour transparency film (50-100 ISO), by Nikon 35mm cameras. These were the Nikon F4s, and F3 HP, lenses used were all Nikkors (16mm, 105mm, 200mm, 600mm, 20mmAF, 200mmAF, 28mmPC). No intentional effort has been made to remove cars or anything that could be considered 'contemporary' or fashionable; this is a British city in the latter part of the 20th century.

Jon Davison is an Oxford based photographer, having moved to Britain from his native New Zealand in 1980.
He specialises in the photography of mood, mainly for Travel and Aviation related work. He often takes risks to get that elusive image, be it land sea or air, home or abroad.
His work is represented worldwide by the Image Bank/Stockphotos Inc, 373 Park Avenue South, New York, NY 10016, USA.